All-American Partner Songs

12 Tremendous Partner Songs for Young Singers

Arranged, with additional Words and Music, by

Sally K. Albrecht

Includes Reproducible Student Pages and Staging Suggestions!

Recording Orchestrated by Tim Hayden

See back cover for CD track numbers.
Note: Reproducible student pages and full-color cover art are included as PDF files on the Enhanced SoundTrax CD.

© 2015 by Alfred Music
All Rights Reserved. Printed in USA.

Book & CD (43436)   ISBN-10: 1-4706-2661-6   ISBN-13: 978-1-4706-2661-7
Teacher's Handbook (43437) ISBN-10: 1-4706-2662-4   ISBN-13: 978-1-4706-2662-4
Enhanced SoundTrax CD (43438)

 Alfred Cares. Contents printed on environmentally responsible paper.

Foreword

For years, teachers and students have enjoyed singing partner songs. There's nothing more fun, and there's no better way to develop independent 2-part singing with your young performers.

All-American Partner Songs offers 12 classic patriotic and folk songs in traditional partner song formats. These well-known favorites will never go out of style! You may choose to have all students learn both parts and then divide the ensemble into two parts to sing both melodies on the final time through the song. Or you may wish to teach Part I only to half of your singers and Part II only to the other half. I have also heard from teachers who combine two different classes or grades together when performing partner songs—one class/grade learns Part I and the other learns Part II.

Staging suggestions are included in the publication where appropriate, both in the full score and in the reproducible student pages. I've tried to keep things interesting yet simple, using primarily upper torso movements. The choreography for "Bill Bailey" is also featured on the choral movement DVD *With a Song!* (43333) and available online at alfred.com/videoondemand. Please note that the Enhanced SoundTrax CD includes PDF files of the reproducible student pages, as well as a full-color version of the cover art.

Enjoy finding new partners and making new friends as you sing these songs!

Sally K. Albrecht

Sally K. Albrecht

Also Available

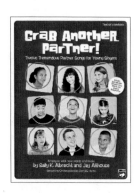

GRAB A PARTNER!
12 Terrific Partner Songs for Young Singers

Book & CD (20174)
Teacher's Handbook (20172)
Enhanced SoundTrax CD (20173)

GRAB ANOTHER PARTNER!
12 Tremendous Partner Songs for Young Singers

Book & CD (21679)
Teacher's Handbook (21677)
Enhanced SoundTrax CD (21678)

BROADWAY PARTNERS!
10 Terrific Partner Songs for Young Singers

Book & CD (39976)
Teacher's Handbook (39974)
Enhanced SoundTrax CD (39975)

POP PARTNERS
10 Tremendous Partner Songs for Young Singers

Book & CD (31232)
Teacher's Handbook (31230)
Enhanced SoundTrax CD (31231)

About the Author

Sally K. Albrecht is a popular choral composer, conductor, and clinician, especially known for her work with choral movement. An annual recipient of the ASCAP Special Music Award since 1987, Sally has more than 450 popular choral publications, over 65 elementary songbooks and musicals, and 16 choral movement instructional DVDs in print. For 24 years, she was the Director of School Choral, Classroom, and Elementary Publications for Alfred Music.

A native of Cleveland, Ohio, Sally received a B.A. Degree from Rollins College (FL) with a double major in Music and Theater. From there she moved to the University of Miami, where she received both an M.A. in Drama and an M.M. in Accompanying. She was an accompanist for Fred Waring and taught in the music departments at Oakland University (MI) and Jersey City State College (NJ).

Sally has worked with literally thousands of teachers, presenting sessions at music conventions and workshops in over 40 states, Canada, Singapore, and Australia. She has directed and staged the half-time show singers performing during two Florida Citrus Bowls, and has conducted hundreds of honor choir events, including festivals at Lincoln Center, Carnegie Hall, and The Kennedy Center.

Sally and her husband, composer and arranger Jay Althouse, currently enjoy living in Raleigh, North Carolina. They were thrilled and honored to have their composition "I Hear America Singing!" performed during the 2009 presidential inauguration ceremonies. Sally currently serves as a Foundation Trustee of the Omicron Delta Kappa national leadership honor society and is a proud recipient of their 2014 Pillar of Leadership Award.

About the Recording

All-American Partner Songs was recorded by Tim Hayden at Ned's Place Recording Studio in Nashville, TN.

Performers include: Jaclyn Brown, Anna Grace Stewart, Hannah Trauscht, and Sarah Valley (lead).

The **Enhanced SoundTrax CD** offers the following:

- Access to both full-performance and accompaniment recordings (on your CD player).

- Downloadable PDF files of the reproducible student pages and the full-color cover art (on your computer). The purchase of this CD carries with it the right to display these images on an interactive whiteboard in the classroom and/or on a school website.

alfred.com/classroom

Please visit our website and browse our interactive Choral and Classroom Catalog at **alfred.com/classroom** to see sample pages, hear audio excerpts (where available), and discover more about all of Alfred Music's elementary musicals, programs, songbooks, classroom resources, and treble chorals.

1. AMERICA
(My Country, 'Tis of Thee)

Words by **SAMUEL FRANCIS SMITH** (1808-1895)

Traditional Melody
Arranged, with additional Words and Music,
by **SALLY K. ALBRECHT**

1st time: PART I *only*
2nd time: PART II *only*
3rd time: Sing both parts

43437

2. AMERICA THE BEAUTIFUL

Words by **KATHARINE LEE BATES** (1859-1929)

Music by **SAMUEL A. WARD** (1874-1903)
Arranged, with additional Words and Music,
by **SALLY K. ALBRECHT**

1st time: PART I only
2nd time: PART II only
3rd time: Sing both parts

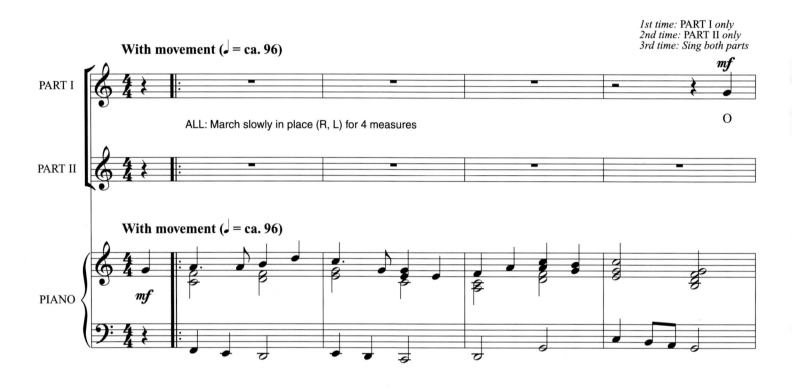

3. BILL BAILEY
(Won't You Come Home?)

Words and Music by **HUGHIE CANNON** (1877-1912)
Arranged, with additional Words and Music,
by **SALLY K. ALBRECHT**

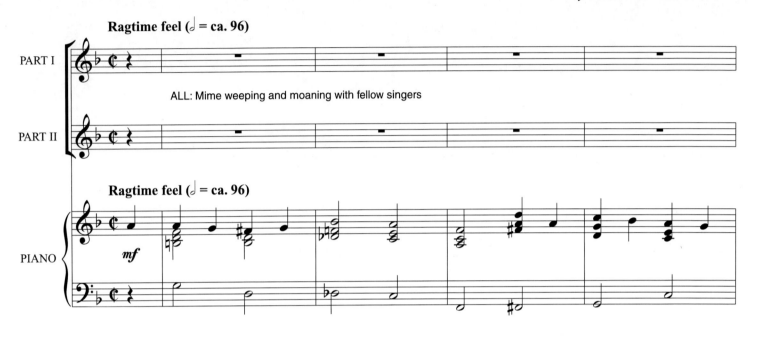

ALL: Mime weeping and moaning with fellow singers

1st time: PART I *only*
2nd time: PART II *only*
3rd time: Sing both parts

PART I: Reach R palm out to R — Pull R fist into heart — R palm out at forehead leaning R

"Won't you come home, Bill Bai - ley, won't you come home?" she moans the

PART II: Wiper sway R, L, R, L — Reach both R — Wiper sway L, R, L, R

"Bill Bai - ley, won't you come home? Bill

43437

4. EV'RY NIGHT WHEN THE SUN GOES IN

Appalachian Folk Song
Arranged, with additional Words and Music,
by **SALLY K. ALBRECHT**

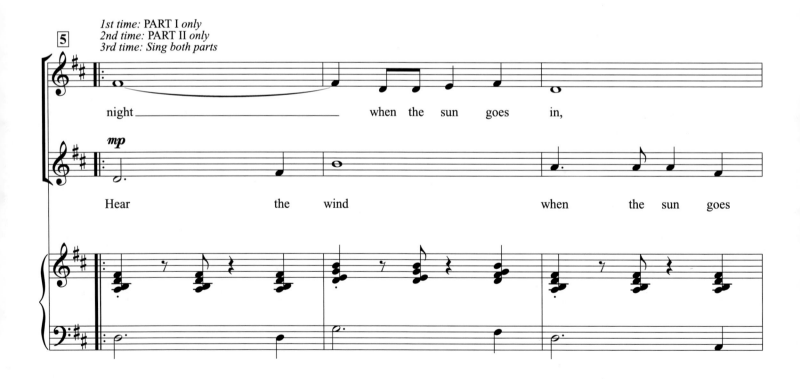

14

43437

5. OH! SUSANNA

Words and Music by
STEPHEN FOSTER (1826-1864)
Arranged, with additional Words and Music,
by **SALLY K. ALBRECHT**

1st time: PART I only
2nd time: PART II only
3rd time: Sing both parts

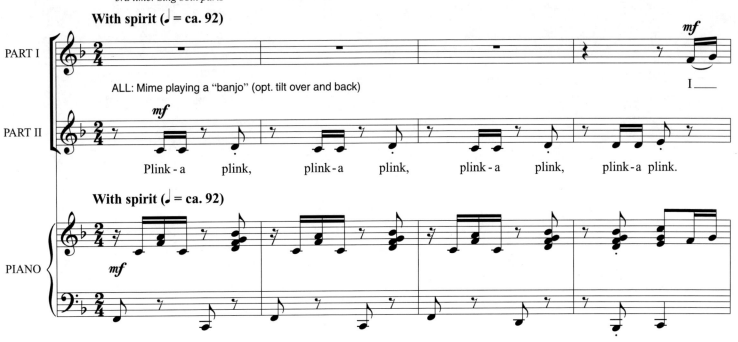

PART I

PART II: ALL: Mime playing a "banjo" (opt. tilt over and back)
Plink-a plink, plink-a plink, plink-a plink, plink-a plink.

PIANO

Lean low to R — Slap R knee w/R out, in, out, in
come from Al - a - bam - a with my ban - jo on my knee. I'm

R to ear (listen) — Play a "banjo"
Can you hear that ban - jo, plink plink-a plink plink, on my knee?

43437

16

43437

6. POLLY WOLLY DOODLE

American Folk Song
Arranged, with additional Words and Music,
by **SALLY K. ALBRECHT**

20

43437

7. SHENANDOAH

American Folk Song
Arranged, with additional Words and Music,
by **SALLY K. ALBRECHT**

1st time: PART I only
2nd time: PART II only
3rd time: Sing both parts

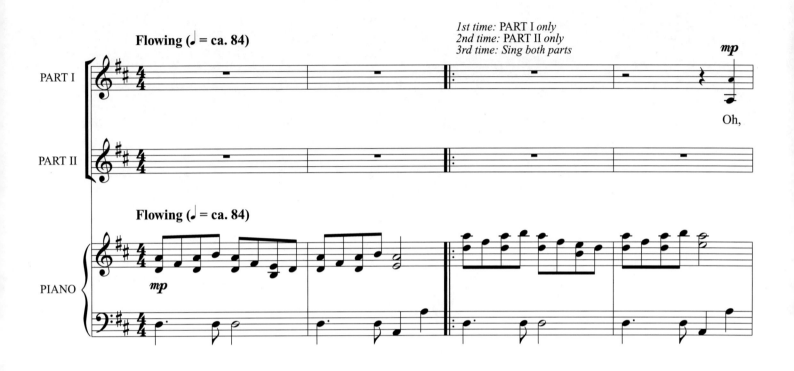

43437

22

43437

8. SIMPLE GIFTS

American Shaker Song
Arranged, with additional Words and Music,
by **SALLY K. ALBRECHT**

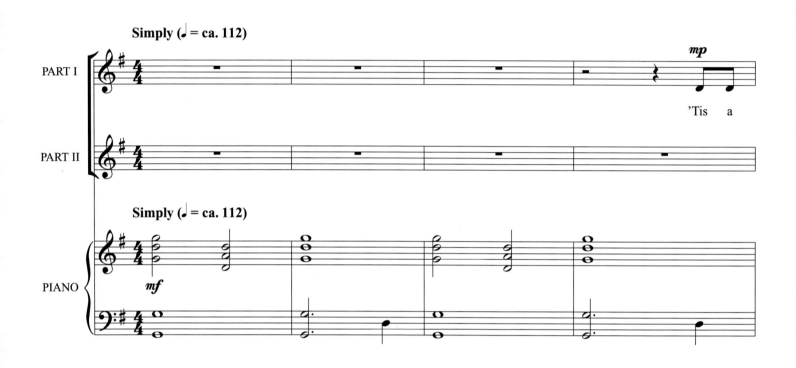

26

43437

9. SWEET BETSY FROM PIKE

American Folk Song
Arranged, with additional Words and Music,
by **SALLY K. ALBRECHT**

43437

10. TAKE ME OUT TO THE BALL GAME

Words by **JACK NORWORTH** (1879-1959)

Music by **ALBERT VON TILZER** (1878-1956)
Arranged, with additional Words and Music,
by **SALLY K. ALBRECHT**

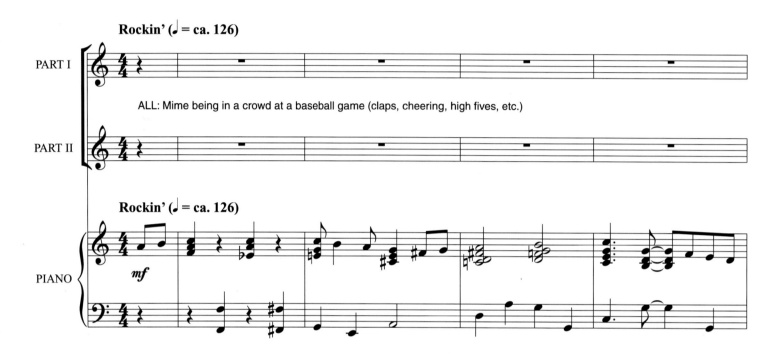

1st time: PART I *only*
2nd time: PART II *only*
3rd time: Sing both parts

11. THE YANKEE DOODLE BOY

Words and Music by **GEORGE M. COHAN** (1878-1942)
Arranged, with additional Words and Music,
by **SALLY K. ALBRECHT**

43437

43437

12. YOU'RE A GRAND OLD FLAG

Words and Music by **GEORGE M. COHAN** (1878-1942)
Arranged, with additional Words and Music,
by **SALLY K. ALBRECHT**

ALL: Mime playing snare drum to rhythm of LH piano through measure 8

CHOREOGRAPHY NOTE: Place an American flag stage right.

38

43437

Reproducible
Student Pages

1. AMERICA
(My Country, 'Tis of Thee)

Words by **SAMUEL FRANCIS SMITH** (1808-1895)

Traditional Melody
Arranged, with additional Words and Music,
by **SALLY K. ALBRECHT**

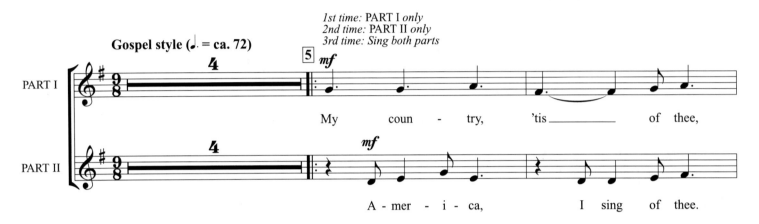

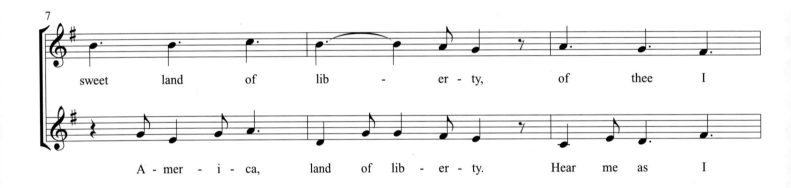

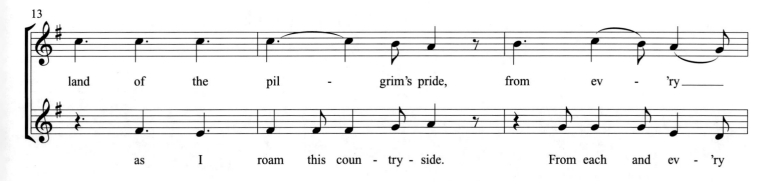

land of the pil - grim's pride, from ev - 'ry

as I roam this coun - try - side. From each and ev - 'ry

moun - tain - side, let freedom ring.

moun - tain - side, let freedom ring.

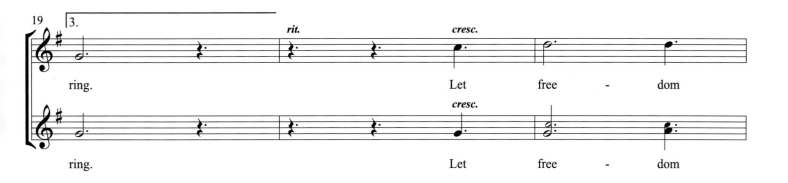

ring. Let free - dom

ring. Let free - dom

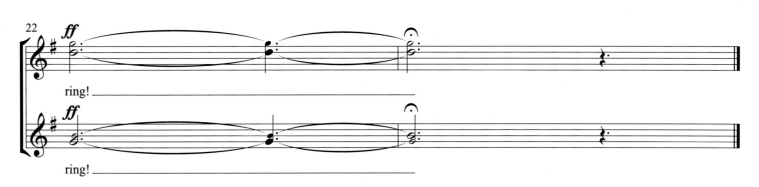

ring!

ring!

2. AMERICA THE BEAUTIFUL

Words by **KATHARINE LEE BATES** (1859-1929)

Music by **SAMUEL A. WARD** (1874-1903)
Arranged, with additional Words and Music,
by **SALLY K. ALBRECHT**

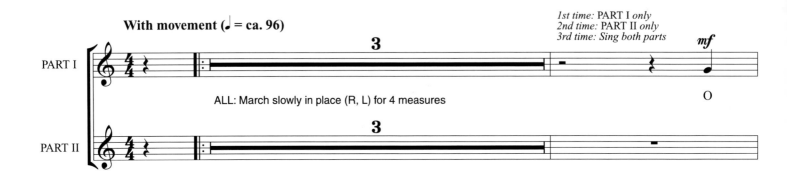

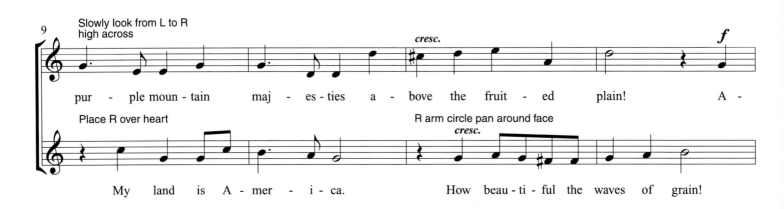

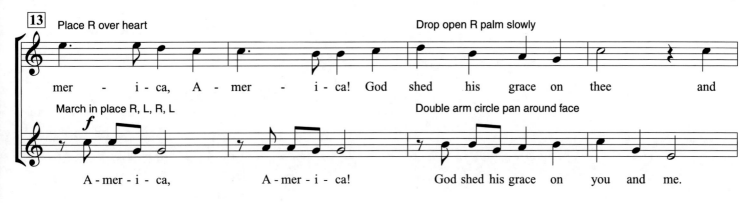

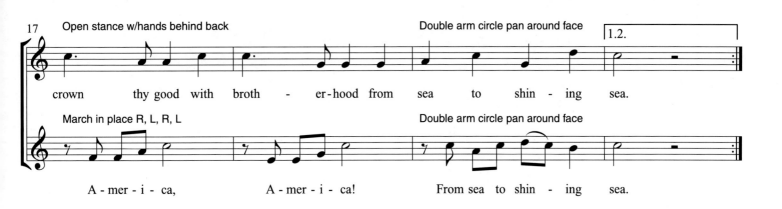

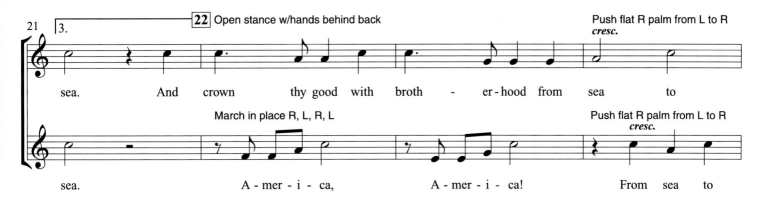

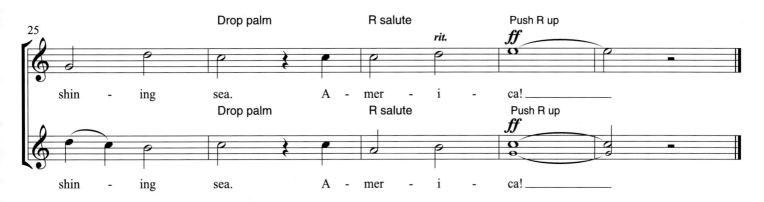

43437

3. BILL BAILEY
(Won't You Come Home?)

Words and Music by **HUGHIE CANNON** (1877-1912)
Arranged, with additional Words and Music,
by **SALLY K. ALBRECHT**

1st time: PART I only
2nd time: PART II only
3rd time: Sing both parts

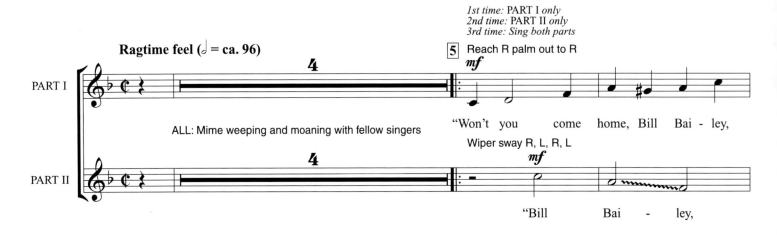

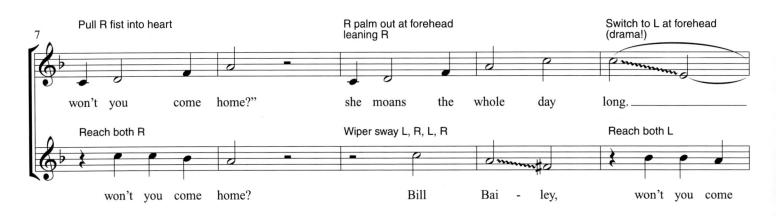

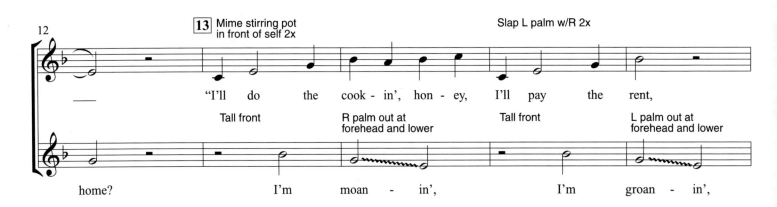

43437

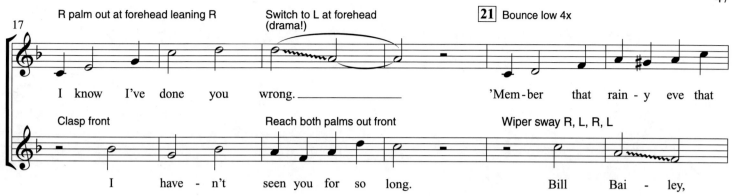

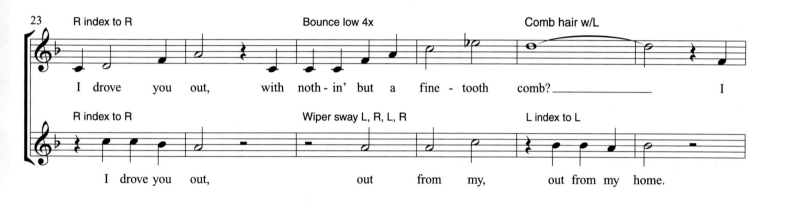

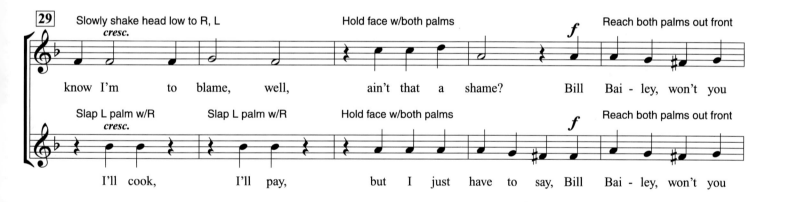

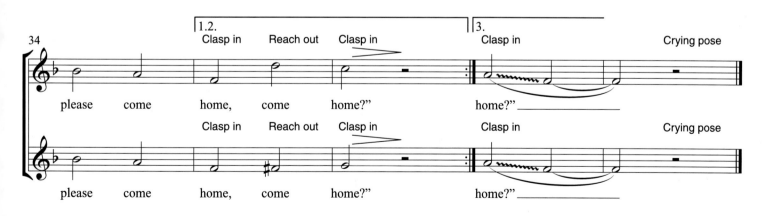

4. EV'RY NIGHT WHEN THE SUN GOES IN

Appalachian Folk Song
Arranged, with additional Words and Music,
by **SALLY K. ALBRECHT**

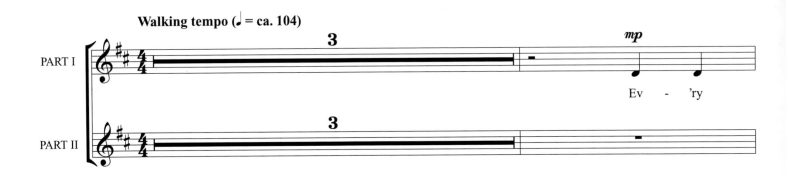

night_____ when the sun goes in, I hang down my

mf

Hear the wind when the sun goes in._____

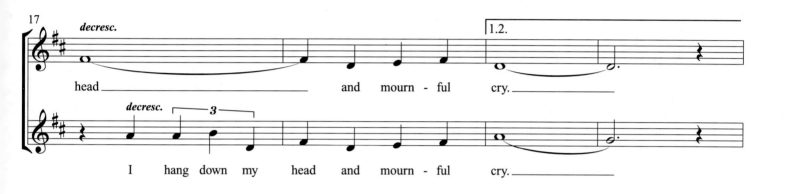

decresc.

head_____ and mourn - ful cry._____

decresc.

I hang down my head and mourn - ful cry._____

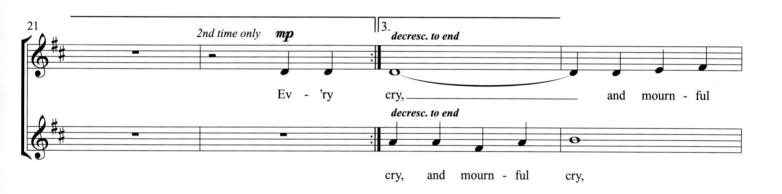

2nd time only **mp**

decresc. to end

Ev - 'ry cry,_____ and mourn - ful

decresc. to end

cry, and mourn - ful cry,

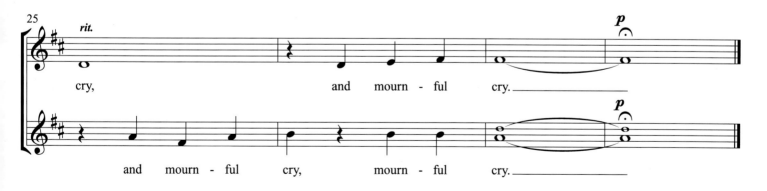

rit. **p**

cry, and mourn - ful cry._____

p

and mourn - ful cry, mourn - ful cry._____

43437

5. OH! SUSANNA

Words and Music by
STEPHEN FOSTER (1826-1864)
Arranged, with additional Words and Music,
by **SALLY K. ALBRECHT**

1st time: PART I *only*
2nd time: PART II *only*
3rd time: Sing both parts

With spirit (♩ = ca. 92)

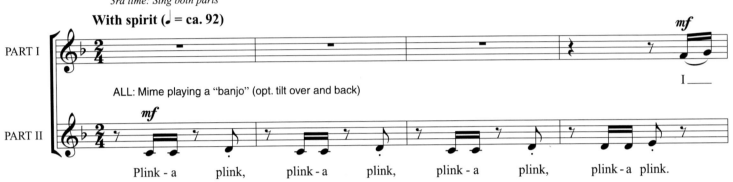

PART I

PART II

ALL: Mime playing a "banjo" (opt. tilt over and back)

Plink - a plink, plink - a plink, plink - a plink, plink - a plink.

I ___

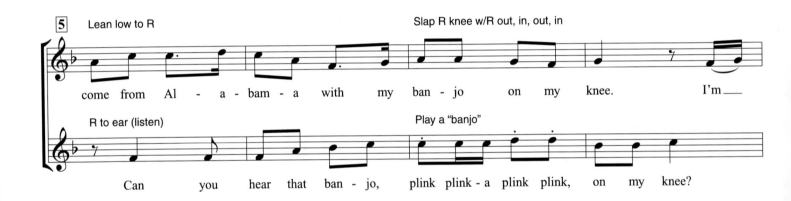

5 Lean low to R · · · Slap R knee w/R out, in, out, in

come from Al - a - bam - a with my ban - jo on my knee. I'm ___

R to ear (listen) · Play a "banjo"

Can you hear that ban - jo, plink plink - a plink plink, on my knee?

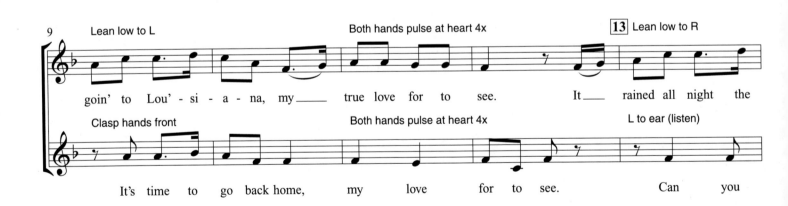

9 Lean low to L · · Both hands pulse at heart 4x · · **13** Lean low to R

goin' to Lou' - si - a - na, my ___ true love for to see. It ___ rained all night the

Clasp hands front · · Both hands pulse at heart 4x · L to ear (listen)

It's time to go back home, my love for to see. Can you

6. POLLY WOLLY DOODLE

American Folk Song
Arranged, with additional Words and Music,
by **SALLY K. ALBRECHT**

43437

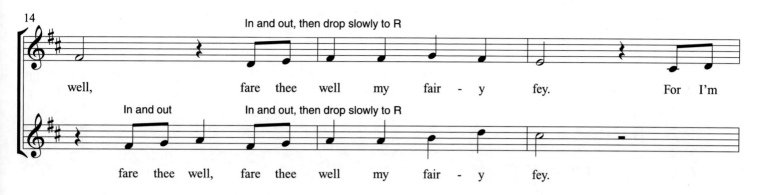

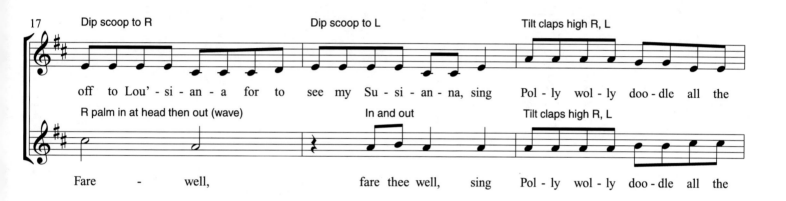

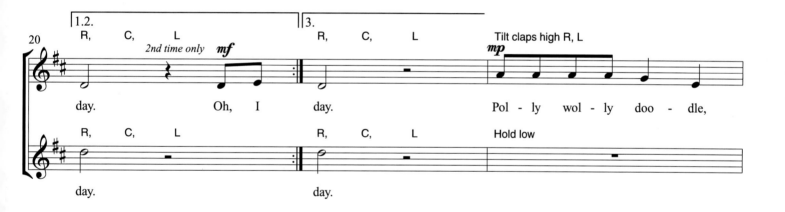

7. SHENANDOAH

American Folk Song
Arranged, with additional Words and Music,
by **SALLY K. ALBRECHT**

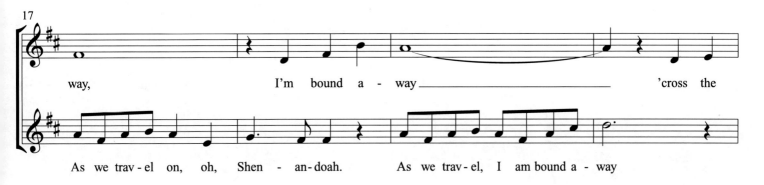

8. SIMPLE GIFTS

American Shaker Song
Arranged, with additional Words and Music,
by **SALLY K. ALBRECHT**

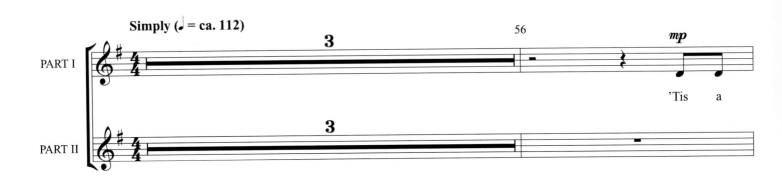

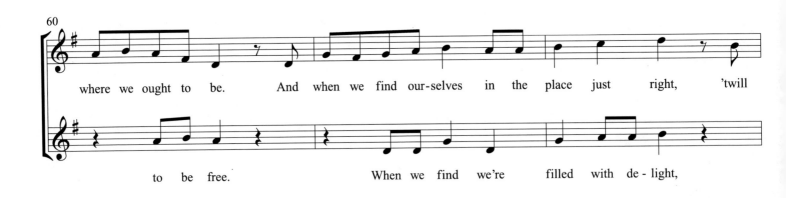

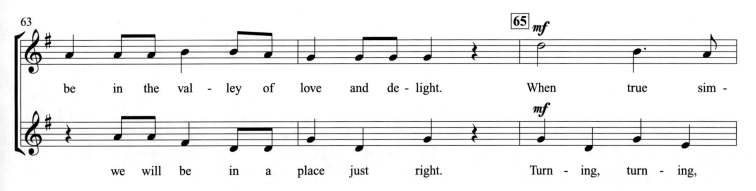

be in the val - ley of love and de - light. When true sim -

we will be in a place just right. Turn - ing, turn - ing,

plic - i - ty is gained, to bow and to bend we shan't be a - shamed. To

turn - ing, turn - ing, turn - ing, turn - ing, we come 'round right.

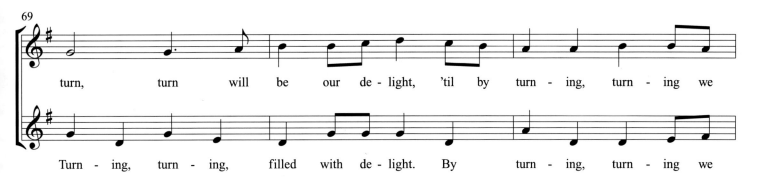

turn, turn will be our de - light, 'til by turn - ing, turn - ing we

Turn - ing, turn - ing, filled with de - light. By turn - ing, turn - ing we

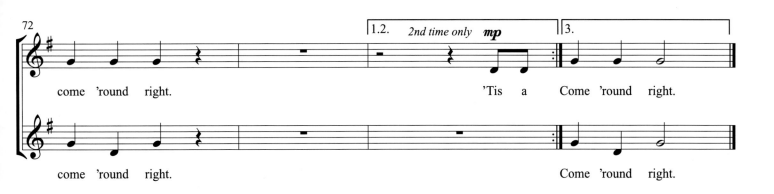

come 'round right. 'Tis a Come 'round right.

come 'round right. Come 'round right.

9. SWEET BETSY FROM PIKE

American Folk Song
Arranged, with additional Words and Music,
by **SALLY K. ALBRECHT**

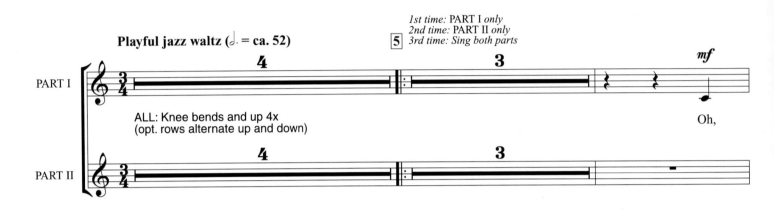

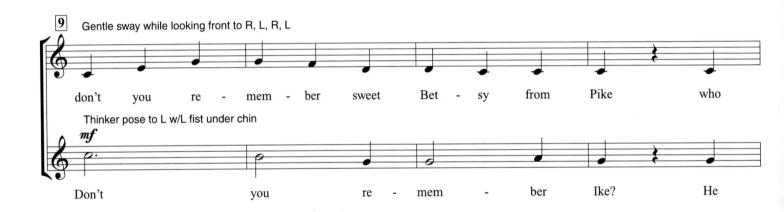

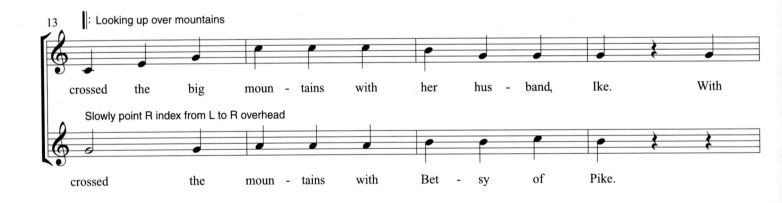

43437

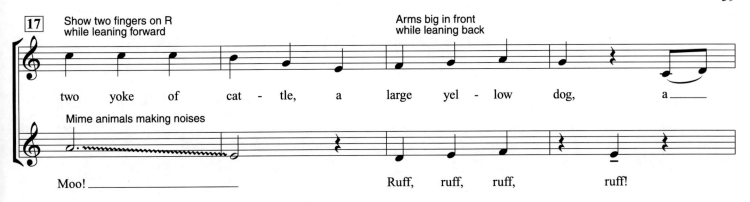

two yoke of cat - tle, a large yel - low dog, a _____

Moo! _____ Ruff, ruff, ruff, ruff!

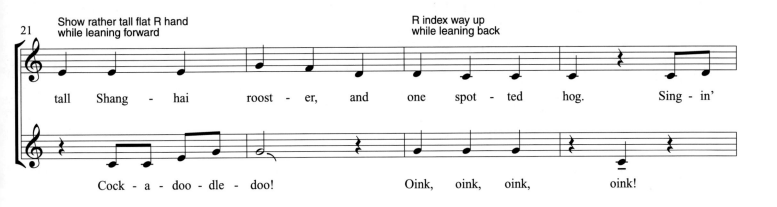

tall Shang - hai roost - er, and one spot - ted hog. Sing - in'

Cock - a - doo - dle - doo! Oink, oink, oink, oink!

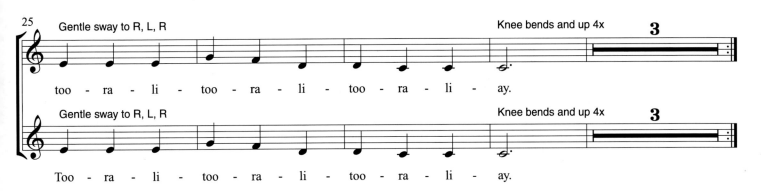

too - ra - li - too - ra - li - too - ra - li - ay.

Too - ra - li - too - ra - li - too - ra - li - ay.

Too - ra - li - too - ra - li - ay!

Too - ra - li - too - ra - li - ay!

10. TAKE ME OUT TO THE BALL GAME

Words by **JACK NORWORTH** (1879-1959)

Music by **ALBERT VON TILZER** (1878-1956)
Arranged, with additional Words and Music,
by **SALLY K. ALBRECHT**

1st time: PART I *only*
2nd time: PART II *only*
3rd time: Sing both parts

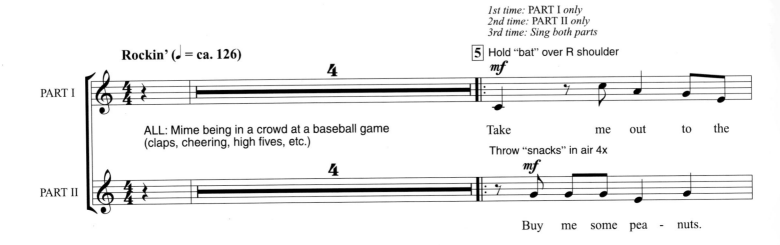

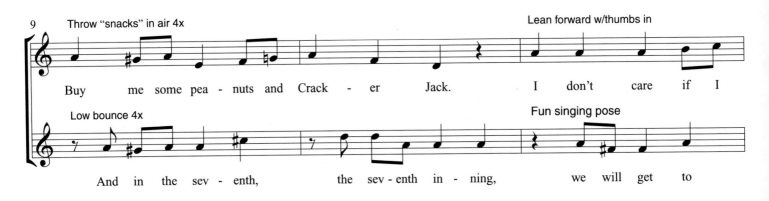

43437

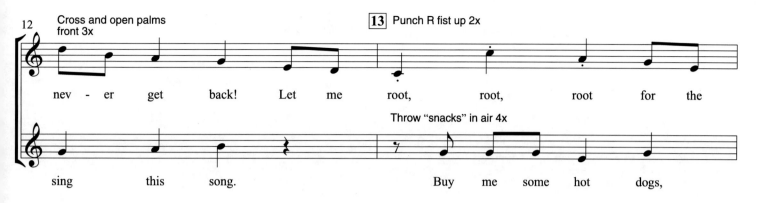

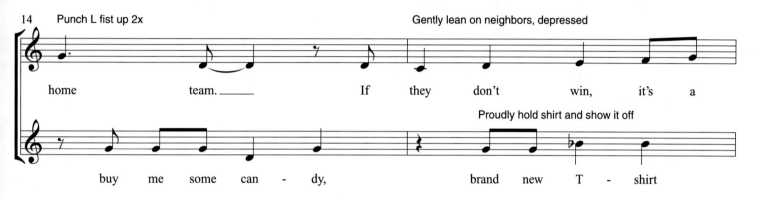

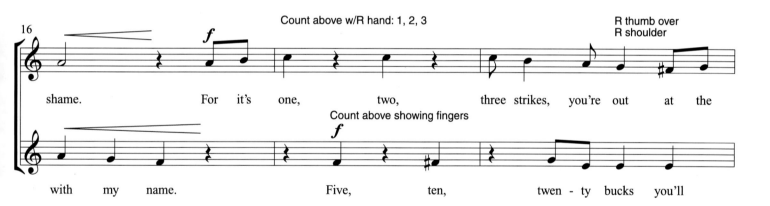

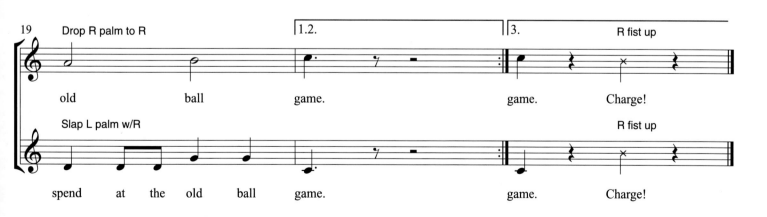

11. THE YANKEE DOODLE BOY

Words and Music by **GEORGE M. COHAN** (1878-1942)
Arranged, with additional Words and Music,
by **SALLY K. ALBRECHT**

12. YOU'RE A GRAND OLD FLAG

Words and Music by **GEORGE M. COHAN** (1878-1942)
Arranged, with additional Words and Music,
by **SALLY K. ALBRECHT**

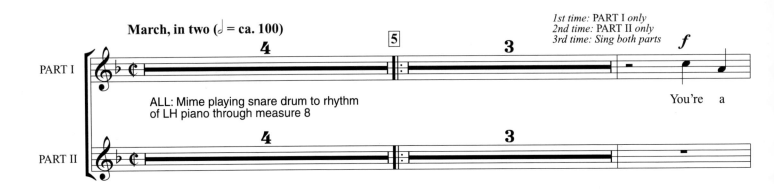

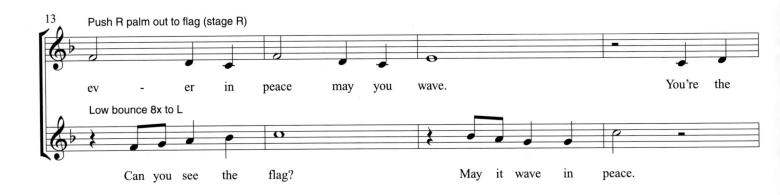

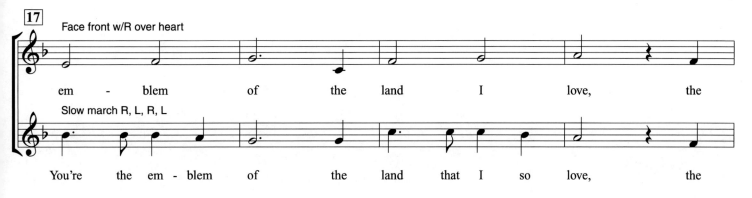

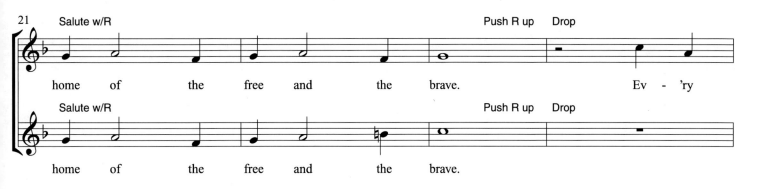

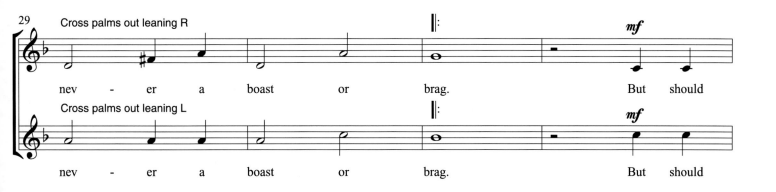

43437

66

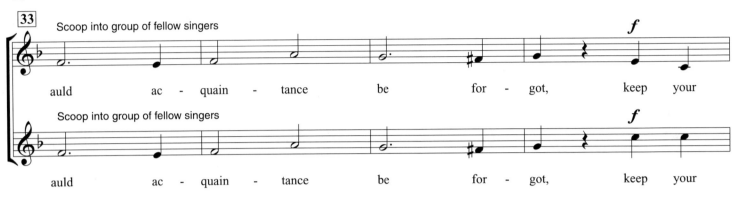

auld ac - quain - tance be for - got, keep your

auld ac - quain - tance be for - got, keep your

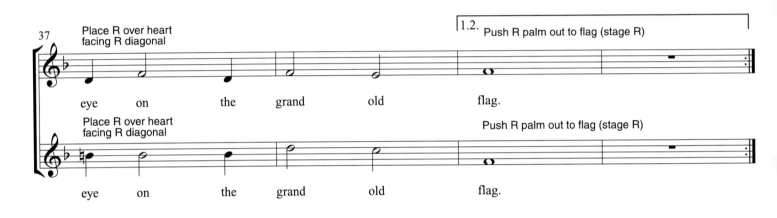

eye on the grand old flag.

eye on the grand old flag.

flag. I love A - mer - i - ca!

flag. I love A - mer - i - ca!

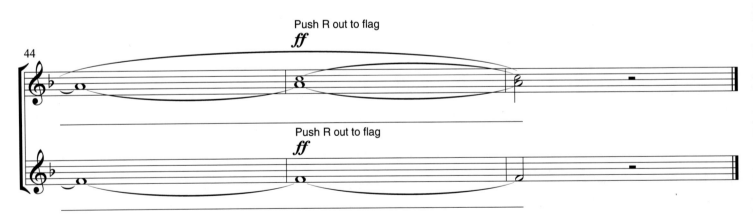

All-American Partner Songs

12 Tremendous Partner Songs for Young Singers

Arranged, with additional Words and Music, by

Sally K. Albrecht

Recording Orchestrated by Tim Hayden